Understanding Financial Fraud's Impact on Victims

C. P. Kumar
Reiki Healer & Author
Roorkee - 247667, India

Disclaimer

While every effort has been made to ensure the accuracy and completeness of the content in this book, the author cannot guarantee that the information contained herein is error-free, up-to-date, or suitable for every individual circumstance.

The author shall not be held liable or responsible for any errors or omissions in the content of the book, nor for any damages, or losses that may arise from any actions taken based upon the suggestions or contents presented in the book.

Readers are advised to use their own judgment and discretion in applying the information provided in this book, and to consult with qualified professionals before taking any action based on the contents of this book. The author disclaims any and all liability or responsibility for any actions taken or not taken based on the information contained in this book.

DEDICATION

To all those whose lives have been disrupted, shattered, or forever changed by the insidious grasp of financial fraud, this book is dedicated to you.

May your stories serve as beacons of understanding, guiding others through the complexities of deception and manipulation.

May your resilience inspire hope in the darkest of times, illuminating pathways to healing and recovery.

May your voices echo loudly, demanding justice, reform, and a future free from the devastating impact of financial fraud.

This dedication is a tribute to your strength, your courage, and your unwavering spirit in the face of adversity.

C. P. Kumar

CONTENTS

PREFACE

Financial fraud is a pervasive and insidious threat that can wreak havoc on the lives of its victims, leaving behind a trail of shattered dreams, broken trust, and profound emotional distress. In the pages of this book, we embark on a journey to understand the multifaceted impact of financial fraud on those who have experienced it firsthand. From the intricate mechanics of various fraud schemes to the devastating aftermath felt by individuals and communities, we explore the depths of this complex issue and shed light on the challenges faced by those who find themselves ensnared in its web.

At the heart of our exploration lies a commitment to unraveling the complexities of financial fraud and its profound repercussions. We begin by examining the myriad forms that fraud can take, from pyramid schemes to identity theft, delving into the mechanics, red flags, and real-life examples that illustrate the devastating consequences for victims. Through this comprehensive overview, readers will gain a deeper understanding of the pervasive nature of financial fraud and the need for heightened vigilance in an increasingly interconnected world.

But beyond the cold calculus of dollars and cents lies the human toll of financial fraud - the emotional, financial, and psychological devastation experienced by its victims. We explore the profound sense of loss and betrayal that accompanies financial ruin, the toll it takes on mental health and relationships, and the stigma and shame that too often silence those who have been defrauded. Through firsthand accounts and expert insights, we shine a light on the often-overlooked aspects of the victim experience, seeking to amplify the voices of those whose lives have been forever altered by fraud.

Yet, amidst the darkness, there are glimmers of resilience and hope. We uncover the coping mechanisms and support systems that help victims navigate the long and arduous road to recovery, advocating for increased financial literacy and empowerment as tools for prevention. We examine the broader community-level impacts of financial fraud, from economic downturns to loss of trust in institutions, and explore the particular vulnerabilities of elderly individuals and marginalized communities. And we call for policy reforms and international cooperation to strengthen enforcement measures and enhance support for fraud victims worldwide.

Ultimately, this book is a testament to the resilience of the human spirit and the power of solidarity in the face of adversity. As we bear witness to the stories of those who have been touched by financial fraud, we are reminded of our shared humanity and our collective responsibility to seek justice and promote healing. Through understanding, empathy, and advocacy, we can begin to dismantle the systems of exploitation that perpetuate financial fraud and build a more just and equitable world for all.

C. P. Kumar
Reiki Healer, Blogger & Author
Former Scientist 'G', National Institute of Hydrology
Roorkee - 247667, India
Web: https://www.angelfire.com/nh/cpkumar/virgo.html

Introduction

Financial fraud has long been a pervasive issue in societies worldwide, leaving devastating impacts on individuals, families, and communities. In the complex landscape of finance, various schemes and tactics are employed by fraudsters to deceive and manipulate unsuspecting victims. Understanding the different types of financial fraud is crucial for both prevention and mitigation efforts. This chapter aims to provide a comprehensive overview of the most prevalent forms of financial fraud, shedding light on their mechanics, characteristics, red flags, and real-life impacts on victims.

Pyramid Schemes

Pyramid schemes lure individuals by promising high returns based on recruiting new participants, rather than selling legitimate products or services. They operate by channeling funds from new investors to earlier ones, with only a select few at the top benefiting. The scheme inevitably collapses when it becomes unsustainable, leaving the majority of participants with significant losses.

Case Study: The infamous "ZeekRewards" scheme, which defrauded investors of over $850 million, exemplifies the devastating consequences of pyramid schemes.

Ponzi Schemes

Similar to pyramid schemes, Ponzi schemes rely on new investors' funds to pay returns to earlier investors, creating the illusion of profitability. However, unlike pyramid schemes, Ponzi schemes typically involve a single orchestrator who fabricates investment returns, leading investors to believe their investments are yielding profits.

Case Study: The Bernie Madoff scandal, one of the largest Ponzi schemes in history, defrauded investors of approximately $65 billion, highlighting the catastrophic impact on victims.

High-Yield Investment Scams

High-yield investment scams promise unrealistically high returns with minimal risk, often targeting inexperienced or financially vulnerable individuals. These schemes often lack transparency and operate without proper regulatory oversight, making it challenging for investors to discern between legitimate opportunities and fraudulent schemes.

Case Study: The "London Capital & Finance" scandal, which preyed on thousands of investors, promising high returns on mini-bonds but ultimately resulting in losses exceeding £236 million.

Insider Trading

Insider trading occurs when individuals with access to non-public information about a company use that information to trade stocks or securities illicitly. This unethical practice undermines market integrity and erodes investor confidence, often resulting in significant financial losses for those unaware of the unfair advantage held by insiders.

Case Study: The Martha Stewart insider trading case, where she was convicted of selling shares based on privileged information, exemplifies the legal and financial ramifications of insider trading.

Securities Fraud

Securities fraud encompasses a range of deceptive practices involving stocks, bonds, or other investment vehicles. This may include false or misleading statements, manipulation of financial reports, or unauthorized trading by brokers. Securities fraud can lead to inflated stock prices, investor losses, and damage to the reputation of affected companies.

Case Study: The Enron scandal, one of the most notorious cases of securities fraud, involved corporate accounting manipulation and led to the bankruptcy of the energy giant, resulting in significant losses for investors and employees alike.

Market Manipulation

Market manipulation involves artificially inflating or deflating the price of securities or commodities to profit from the resulting price movements. Techniques such as spreading false rumors, engaging in wash trading, or cornering the market are used to manipulate supply and demand dynamics for financial gain.

Wash trading is a form of market manipulation where a trader simultaneously buys and sells the same financial instruments to create the illusion of activity, without any change in ownership, in order to manipulate prices or volume.

: The "Wolf of Wall Street" Jordan Belfort's manipulation of penny stocks through pump-and-dump schemes illustrates the destructive impact of market manipulation on unsuspecting investors.

Pump-and-dump schemes involve artificially inflating the price of a stock through misleading statements or promotions, followed by selling off shares at the inflated price for profit, leaving unsuspecting investors with worthless holdings.

Accounting Fraud

Accounting fraud involves deliberately misrepresenting financial information to deceive investors, regulators, or other stakeholders. This may include inflating revenues, understating expenses, or hiding liabilities to create a false perception of a company's financial health. Accounting fraud can lead to inflated stock prices, shareholder lawsuits, and regulatory sanctions.

Case Study: The WorldCom scandal, where the telecommunications giant overstated profits by billions of dollars through fraudulent accounting practices, resulting in one of the largest bankruptcies in U.S. history.

Churning and Unauthorized Trading

Churning occurs when brokers excessively trade securities in a client's account to generate commissions, often without the client's consent. Unauthorized trading involves executing trades without proper authorization from the client, leading to unnecessary risks and financial losses for investors.

Case Study: The unauthorized trading scandal at the now-defunct brokerage firm "Barings Bank", orchestrated by rogue trader Nick Leeson, resulted in losses exceeding $1.4 billion and the bank's collapse.

Fee Padding

Fee padding involves charging excessive or undisclosed fees to clients for financial services, such as investment management or brokerage services. This deceptive practice erodes investor returns and undermines trust in financial institutions.

Case Study: The Wells Fargo fake account scandal, where employees opened millions of unauthorized accounts to meet sales targets, highlights the ethical and legal implications of fee padding.

Mortgage Fraud

Mortgage fraud encompasses various schemes aimed at deceiving lenders, borrowers, or investors in the mortgage lending process. This may include falsifying income or assets, inflating property values, or submitting fraudulent documentation to obtain loans under false pretenses.

Case Study: The subprime mortgage crisis of 2008, fueled by widespread mortgage fraud and predatory lending practices, resulted in a global financial meltdown and the foreclosure of millions of homes.

Identity Theft and Phishing Scams

Identity theft involves stealing personal information to commit financial fraud, such as opening unauthorized accounts or making fraudulent purchases. Phishing scams lure individuals into disclosing sensitive information, such as passwords or credit card numbers, through deceptive emails, websites, or phone calls.

Case Study: The Equifax data breach, where hackers gained access to sensitive personal information of over 147 million people, underscores the pervasive threat of identity theft and cybersecurity breaches.

Cybersecurity Breaches

Cybersecurity breaches involve unauthorized access to computer systems or networks to steal sensitive information or disrupt operations. These breaches can lead to financial losses, reputational damage, and legal liabilities for affected individuals and organizations.

Case Study: The ransomware attack on Colonial Pipeline, one of the largest fuel pipeline operators in the U.S., disrupted fuel supplies and resulted in a ransom payment of $4.4 million to hackers.

Money Laundering

Money laundering involves disguising the origins of illegally obtained funds through a series of complex financial transactions. This facilitates the integration of illicit funds into the legitimate economy, enabling criminals to profit from their illegal activities while evading detection by authorities.

Case Study: The "Russian Laundromat", a vast money laundering scheme involving approximately $20 billion, highlights the global scale and sophistication of money laundering operations.

Conclusion

Financial fraud encompasses a diverse range of schemes and tactics aimed at deceiving and defrauding unsuspecting victims. From pyramid schemes and Ponzi schemes to insider trading and money laundering, the impact of financial fraud extends far beyond financial losses, often resulting in emotional distress, legal battles, and shattered trust. By understanding the mechanics and red flags associated with different types of financial fraud, individuals can better protect themselves and their assets from falling victim to these deceptive practices. Additionally, policymakers and regulators play a crucial role in implementing measures to combat financial fraud and safeguard the integrity of financial markets.

Introduction

Financial fraud is not merely a crime against finances; it's an assault on the very fabric of trust and security. Behind every fraudulent transaction, there lies a victim grappling with a myriad of emotions, financial distress, and psychological trauma. Understanding the victim experience is paramount in comprehending the profound impact financial fraud inflicts on individuals and communities alike.

Unveiling the Emotional Turmoil

The emotional rollercoaster that victims of financial fraud endure is unparalleled. Shock and disbelief often mark the initial reaction upon discovering the deception. Trust, meticulously built over years, shatters in an instant, leaving victims feeling betrayed and vulnerable. Anger, directed towards both the perpetrator and oneself for falling prey, simmers beneath the surface. Shame and embarrassment compound the emotional burden, as victims grapple with feelings of inadequacy and self-blame. The sense of violation transcends mere monetary loss, penetrating the very essence of one's being.

Navigating Financial Ruin

Financial fraud exacts a heavy toll on victims' financial well-being, often plunging them into a downward spiral of debt and destitution. Savings painstakingly accumulated over years vanish in the blink of an eye, leaving victims financially crippled. The repercussions extend far beyond immediate losses, as victims struggle to rebuild their financial lives amidst mounting bills and depleted resources. Credit scores plummet, hindering access to loans and other financial lifelines. The road to financial recovery is fraught with challenges, with some victims facing the grim reality of bankruptcy and foreclosure. The financial scars of fraud linger long after the fraudulent transactions cease, casting a shadow of uncertainty over victims' futures.

The Psychological Fallout

Beyond the tangible losses lies the invisible wounds inflicted by financial fraud – the psychological trauma that leaves lasting scars on victims' mental well-being. Anxiety and stress become constant companions as victims grapple with the uncertainty of their financial futures. Sleepless nights are spent wrestling with intrusive thoughts and crippling fear. Depression often sets in, as victims struggle to come to terms with the magnitude of their losses and the perceived sense of helplessness. Trust, once shattered, proves difficult to rebuild, leading to heightened skepticism and paranoia in future financial dealings. The psychological toll of financial fraud reverberates through every facet of victims' lives, eroding their sense of security and robbing them of peace of mind.

Coping Mechanisms and Support

In the aftermath of financial fraud, victims often find solace in connecting with others who have shared similar experiences. Support groups and counseling services offer a lifeline for those navigating the turbulent waters of recovery. Sharing stories and lending a sympathetic ear can help alleviate feelings of isolation and shame. Practical assistance in navigating legal and financial hurdles empowers victims to reclaim a sense of control over their lives. Cultivating resilience and fostering a sense of hope are essential in rebuilding shattered lives and moving forward in the face of adversity.

Prevention and Advocacy

While the repercussions of financial fraud are undeniably devastating, efforts to prevent future victimization and advocate for change are paramount. Education and awareness play a crucial role in equipping individuals with the knowledge and tools to recognize and avoid fraudulent schemes. Empowering consumers to safeguard their financial information and exercise due diligence in their transactions can help stem the tide of fraud. Advocacy efforts aimed at strengthening regulations and enforcement mechanisms serve to hold perpetrators accountable and protect vulnerable populations from exploitation. By uniting in the fight against financial fraud, we can strive towards a future where individuals are empowered to safeguard their financial well-being and trust is restored in the integrity of financial systems.

Conclusion

The victim experience of financial fraud is characterized by profound emotional, financial, and psychological turmoil. From the initial shock of betrayal to the long road of recovery, victims grapple with a myriad of challenges that extend far beyond mere monetary loss. Understanding the multifaceted impact of financial fraud is essential in fostering empathy and support for those affected and in driving efforts to prevent future victimization. By shedding light on the victim experience, we can work towards creating a more just and equitable financial landscape where trust is upheld, and individuals are empowered to safeguard their financial futures.

Introduction

Financial fraud is a pervasive threat in today's world, leaving victims not only emotionally shattered but also grappling with the immediate impact of financial ruin. The consequences of falling victim to fraud extend far beyond mere monetary losses; they permeate every aspect of the victim's life, shattering their financial stability and leaving them struggling to cope with sudden and often devastating setbacks.

The Shock of Betrayal

The initial blow of financial fraud is often the shock of betrayal. Victims, whether individuals or businesses, find themselves blindsided by the discovery that someone they trusted has violated that trust for personal gain. This betrayal amplifies the sense of violation and adds a layer of emotional turmoil to the already distressing experience of financial loss.

Sudden Losses and Unforeseen Expenses

The immediate impact of financial fraud is felt in the sudden and substantial losses incurred by the victim. Whether it's through embezzlement, identity theft, or investment scams, the fraudster's actions can wipe out savings, retirement funds, and even entire businesses in one fell swoop. Moreover, victims are often left to deal with unforeseen expenses, such as legal fees, credit monitoring services, and restitution payments, further exacerbating their financial distress.

Struggling to Make Ends Meet

With their financial resources depleted, victims of fraud find themselves struggling to make ends meet. They may face difficulties paying bills, servicing debts, or even putting food on the table. The sudden loss of income or assets can plunge individuals and families into financial crisis, forcing them to make difficult decisions about priorities and sacrifices.

Damage to Credit and Reputation

Financial fraud can also wreak havoc on the victim's credit and reputation. Fraudulent activity, such as unauthorized credit card charges or falsified loans, can tarnish the victim's credit history and make it difficult, if not impossible, to secure future loans or lines of credit. Moreover, the stigma of being a fraud victim may damage the victim's reputation personally and professionally, leading to social isolation and career setbacks.

Emotional and Psychological Toll

Beyond the tangible losses, financial fraud exacts a heavy emotional and psychological toll on its victims. The stress, anxiety, and feelings of betrayal can manifest in a myriad of ways, including depression, insomnia, and even physical health problems. Victims may struggle to trust others or feel a sense of shame and embarrassment about their situation, further compounding their emotional distress.

Strained Relationships

The fallout from financial fraud can strain relationships with family, friends, and colleagues. The stress of dealing with the aftermath of fraud can lead to conflicts and misunderstandings, as victims may withdraw or lash out in frustration. Moreover, financial strains can strain partnerships and marriages, as couples grapple with the financial fallout and the emotional toll it takes on their relationship.

Legal Battles and Uncertain Futures

Navigating the legal aftermath of financial fraud can be a long and arduous process for victims. They may find themselves embroiled in legal battles with the fraudster, financial institutions, or government agencies, adding further stress and uncertainty to an already difficult situation. Moreover, the outcome of these legal proceedings is often uncertain, leaving victims in limbo about their financial future.

Seeking Support and Recovery

In the wake of financial fraud, victims often turn to various sources of support and resources to help them cope and recover. This may include seeking counseling or therapy to address the emotional trauma, reaching out to support groups or advocacy organizations for guidance and solidarity, or enlisting the help of financial advisors and legal experts to navigate the complexities of their situation.

Conclusion

The immediate impact of financial fraud is profound and far-reaching, leaving victims reeling from the sudden upheaval of their financial stability and grappling with the emotional fallout of betrayal and loss. However, amidst the devastation, there is hope for recovery and resilience. By seeking support, resources, and taking proactive steps to rebuild their lives, victims can eventually emerge from the ashes of financial ruin stronger and more resilient than ever before.

Chapter 4. Emotional Distress and Mental Health

Introduction

Financial fraud not only results in monetary losses but also inflicts severe emotional distress and mental health implications on its victims. Beyond the tangible consequences, such as loss of savings or assets, victims often grapple with profound psychological challenges. This article delves into the intricate relationship between financial fraud and mental health, exploring the manifestations of emotional distress, including depression, anxiety, and trauma.

Understanding Emotional Distress

Financial fraud shatters the sense of security and trust that individuals have in the world around them. Victims often experience a myriad of emotions ranging from shock and disbelief to anger and shame. The sudden realization of being deceived and manipulated can lead to a profound sense of betrayal, exacerbating the emotional turmoil. Moreover, the loss of financial stability can evoke feelings of helplessness and vulnerability, further intensifying the distress.

Depression: A Silent Struggle

One of the most prevalent mental health consequences of financial fraud is depression. The weight of financial losses coupled with the sense of powerlessness can plunge victims into a state of profound sadness and hopelessness. The constant worry about financial security and the inability to trust others can lead to persistent feelings of despair. Victims may withdraw from social interactions, experience changes in appetite or sleep patterns, and struggle to find joy in activities they once enjoyed. The stigma associated with being defrauded may prevent individuals from seeking help, exacerbating their isolation and deepening the grip of depression.

Anxiety: The Perpetual State of Fear

Anxiety often becomes a constant companion for victims of financial fraud. The uncertainty surrounding their financial future, coupled with the fear of being targeted again, can trigger debilitating levels of anxiety. Victims may experience heightened levels of stress, panic attacks, and an overwhelming sense of apprehension. Simple tasks such as checking emails or answering phone calls may induce feelings of dread, as they fear encountering reminders of their victimization. The persistent fear of losing control over their finances or falling prey to further deceit can significantly impair their ability to function on a day-to-day basis.

Trauma: The Lingering Impact

Financial fraud can inflict deep emotional wounds that resemble the aftermath of traumatic events. The sense of violation and loss of trust can leave lasting scars on the psyche of the victims. Many individuals report experiencing symptoms akin to post-traumatic stress disorder (PTSD), such as intrusive thoughts, flashbacks, and hypervigilance. The trauma of being defrauded can disrupt their sense of safety and stability, leading to profound changes in their worldview. Even long after the fraud has occurred, the trauma continues to reverberate, influencing their relationships, decision-making, and overall well-being.

Coping Mechanisms and Recovery

Coping with the emotional aftermath of financial fraud requires a multifaceted approach that addresses both the practical and psychological aspects of recovery. Seeking support from loved ones, friends, or support groups can provide a crucial lifeline for victims, helping them feel less isolated and alone in their struggles. Professional therapy or counseling can also play a pivotal role in helping individuals process their emotions, develop coping strategies, and regain a sense of control over their lives. Additionally, engaging in self-care activities such as exercise, mindfulness, and hobbies can help alleviate symptoms of depression and anxiety, fostering resilience in the face of adversity.

Preventive Measures and Advocacy

In addition to supporting victims in their journey towards healing, it is imperative to advocate for preventive measures that mitigate the risk of financial fraud. Educating the public about common scams, warning signs, and protective measures can empower individuals to safeguard themselves against potential threats. Furthermore, holding perpetrators of financial fraud accountable through legal channels sends a clear message that such actions will not be tolerated. By raising awareness and advocating for systemic changes, we can work towards creating a safer and more secure environment for all individuals.

Conclusion

Financial fraud exacts a heavy toll not only on victims' financial well-being but also on their mental health and emotional stability. Depression, anxiety, and trauma are among the profound psychological consequences that individuals may endure in the aftermath of being defrauded. Recognizing and addressing these mental health implications is essential for supporting victims on their journey towards healing and recovery. By fostering empathy, providing resources, and advocating for preventive measures, we can work towards creating a more resilient and compassionate society where victims of financial fraud are not only acknowledged but also supported in their pursuit of justice and healing.

Introduction

Financial fraud is not merely a crime of numbers and deceit; it's a malevolent force that corrodes trust and fractures relationships. The ramifications extend far beyond financial loss, delving into the realms of emotional distress and interpersonal turmoil. In this discourse, we delve into the intricate web of strained relationships stemming from financial fraud, exploring its profound impact on families, friendships, and business associations.

Understanding Financial Fraud

Financial fraud encompasses a spectrum of deceptive practices aimed at illicitly obtaining money or assets. From Ponzi schemes to identity theft, perpetrators exploit vulnerabilities for personal gain, leaving a trail of devastation in their wake. Victims, often blindsided by the cunning schemes, grapple with the aftermath, confronting not only financial ruin but also the erosion of trust and stability in their relationships.

The Toll on Family Dynamics

Within the fabric of familial bonds, financial fraud inflicts deep wounds that may never fully heal. Betrayal by a spouse or family member engenders a profound sense of betrayal and shattered trust. The once-solid foundation of love and support crumbles under the weight of deceit, leaving behind a landscape of resentment and bitterness. Financial strain exacerbates tensions, pitting loved ones against each other in a desperate struggle for survival. Children, innocent bystanders in the tumultuous aftermath, bear the brunt of familial discord, grappling with the emotional fallout and fractured family dynamics.

Consider the Smiths, a quintessential American family ensnared in the web of financial fraud. What began as an investment opportunity touted by a trusted friend spiraled into a nightmare of deceit and loss. As the truth unraveled, so too did the bonds of trust within the family. Resentment festered as blame was apportioned, leading to bitter arguments and estrangement. The once-close-knit family found themselves adrift in a sea of uncertainty, grappling with the fallout of shattered dreams and broken promises.

Navigating Friendships Amidst Betrayal

Friendships, built on a foundation of mutual trust and camaraderie, are not immune to the corrosive effects of financial fraud. The revelation of deceit leaves victims reeling, grappling with feelings of betrayal and disbelief. Trusted confidants are unmasked as perpetrators, leaving behind a trail of shattered trust and fractured friendships. The social fabric unravels as victims withdraw, grappling with feelings of shame and embarrassment. Isolation sets in as once-vibrant social circles dwindle, leaving behind a void of loneliness and distrust.

Case Study: Sarah's Struggle

Sarah, a vivacious social butterfly with a wide circle of friends, found herself grappling with the aftermath of financial fraud. A close friend turned out to be the mastermind behind a Ponzi scheme, leaving Sarah reeling with shock and disbelief. The betrayal cut deep, leaving behind a trail of broken trust and shattered friendships. As news of the scandal spread, Sarah found herself ostracized by former friends, grappling with feelings of isolation and distrust. The once-vibrant socialite retreated into a shell of loneliness, navigating the turbulent waters of betrayal and deceit.

The Fallout in Business Relationships

In the realm of business, trust and integrity form the bedrock of successful partnerships. Financial fraud, however, undermines these principles, leaving behind a trail of broken contracts and shattered reputations. Business associates, once united in pursuit of common goals, find themselves embroiled in legal battles and financial turmoil. Trust evaporates as suspicion reigns supreme, leading to the dissolution of partnerships and alliances. The fallout extends beyond the boardroom, permeating every facet of professional life and leaving behind a legacy of distrust and betrayal.

Case Study: The Corporate Catastrophe

Consider the corporate catastrophe that unfolded at XYZ Enterprises, a thriving business brought to its knees by financial fraud. What began as a lucrative partnership with a trusted vendor devolved into a nightmare of deceit and deception. As the truth emerged, so too did the cracks in the foundation of trust that once held the company together. Legal battles ensued, tarnishing the company's reputation and eroding investor confidence. Business associates, once allies, turned adversaries, embroiled in a bitter struggle for restitution and justice.

Conclusion

Financial fraud exacts a heavy toll not only in terms of financial loss but also in its profound impact on relationships. From strained family dynamics to fractured friendships and business alliances, the fallout extends far beyond monetary considerations. Navigating through the wreckage of shattered trust and broken bonds requires resilience, empathy, and a steadfast commitment to rebuilding what has been lost. As we confront the aftermath of financial fraud, let us not forget the human cost - the shattered lives and fractured relationships left in its wake.

Introduction

In today's interconnected world, trust forms the cornerstone of our interactions with various institutions, particularly financial ones. However, when individuals fall prey to financial fraud, the repercussions extend far beyond mere monetary loss. Victims often find themselves grappling not just with the financial ramifications but also with the profound erosion of trust in the very institutions meant to safeguard their assets. This article delves into the intricate dynamics of trust and its gradual dissolution in the wake of financial fraud, shedding light on the multifaceted impact it leaves on victims.

Understanding Trust

Trust is a delicate construct, built over time through a combination of reliability, integrity, and competence. In the realm of finance, individuals place their trust in a myriad of institutions, including banks, investment firms, and regulatory bodies, entrusting them with their hard-earned savings and investments. This trust forms the bedrock of the financial system, fostering stability and facilitating economic growth. However, when this trust is violated through fraudulent activities, the consequences reverberate far beyond the immediate victims.

Erosion of Trust in Financial Institutions

Financial fraud shatters the illusion of security that individuals associate with traditional banking institutions. Whether it's through elaborate Ponzi schemes or sophisticated cybercrimes, perpetrators exploit vulnerabilities in the system, leaving victims disillusioned and distrustful. The betrayal of trust by financial institutions not only undermines their credibility but also leaves a lasting impact on the victims' psyche. The sense of betrayal and vulnerability experienced by victims often lingers long after the fraud has been uncovered, casting a shadow of doubt over their future financial dealings.

Impact on Trust in Government Agencies

Government agencies tasked with regulating the financial sector play a crucial role in maintaining market integrity and investor confidence. However, instances of regulatory failures or perceived complicity in fraudulent activities can severely undermine trust in these institutions. When victims of financial fraud perceive a lack of accountability or responsiveness from government agencies, their faith in the system is further eroded. The failure to effectively investigate and prosecute fraudsters not only perpetuates a sense of injustice but also fosters a culture of impunity, eroding trust in the regulatory framework.

Role of Regulatory Bodies

Regulatory bodies such as the Securities and Exchange Commission (SEC) or the Financial Industry Regulatory Authority (FINRA) are entrusted with safeguarding investors' interests and maintaining the integrity of financial markets. However, instances of regulatory capture or lax enforcement can shake the foundations of trust in these institutions. When victims of financial fraud witness regulatory failures or perceive a lack of transparency in the regulatory process, their confidence in the system is significantly undermined. The disconnect between regulatory rhetoric and on-the-ground realities further deepens the sense of betrayal experienced by victims, exacerbating the erosion of trust.

Psychological Impact of Financial Fraud

Beyond the tangible financial losses, financial fraud inflicts profound psychological wounds on its victims. The sense of betrayal and violation experienced by individuals undermines their faith in the institutions meant to protect them, fostering feelings of vulnerability and helplessness. Victims often grapple with a range of emotions, including anger, shame, and self-doubt, as they come to terms with the extent of the deception. The erosion of trust in financial institutions and regulatory bodies can lead to a pervasive sense of cynicism and distrust, permeating every aspect of the victims' lives.

Rebuilding Trust and Restoring Confidence

Rebuilding trust in the aftermath of financial fraud is a complex and arduous process that requires concerted efforts from both institutions and policymakers. Transparency, accountability, and effective enforcement of regulations are essential for restoring confidence in the financial system. Empowering victims through access to support services and restitution mechanisms can help mitigate the psychological toll of fraud and instill a sense of justice. Additionally, enhancing financial literacy and awareness can empower individuals to make informed decisions and protect themselves from falling victim to future fraud.

Conclusion

Financial fraud not only exacts a tangible toll on its victims but also leaves behind a trail of shattered trust and broken confidence. The erosion of trust in financial institutions, government agencies, and regulatory bodies undermines the very fabric of the financial system, threatening its stability and integrity. As we strive to combat financial fraud and protect vulnerable investors, it is imperative to recognize the profound impact it has on trust and work towards rebuilding confidence in the institutions meant to safeguard our financial well-being. Only through concerted efforts to address the root causes of fraud and restore faith in the system can we begin to heal the wounds inflicted by financial deceit.

Introduction

Financial fraud inflicts more than just monetary losses; it leaves a lasting impact on victims, often extending beyond the realm of finances into emotional and psychological domains. Understanding the complexities of recovery is crucial in addressing the needs of those affected by financial fraud. This article delves into the challenges victims face in recovering financially and emotionally from the aftermath of fraud.

Financial Fallout

Financial fraud can devastate victims financially, wiping out savings, investments, and even retirement funds in one fell swoop. Victims may find themselves grappling with immense debt, damaged credit scores, and the daunting task of rebuilding their financial security from scratch. The process of reclaiming stolen assets or seeking restitution can be arduous, often leading to prolonged financial strain.

Legal Battles

Navigating the legal system to seek justice and restitution can be an uphill battle for fraud victims. Legal proceedings may be protracted and costly, requiring victims to invest significant time, energy, and financial resources into pursuing their case. Moreover, the outcome of legal proceedings is uncertain, leaving victims in a state of limbo and exacerbating their sense of vulnerability and helplessness.

Emotional Toll

The emotional toll of financial fraud can be profound, causing feelings of betrayal, anger, shame, and anxiety. Victims may experience a loss of trust in others, including financial institutions and authority figures, leading to a heightened sense of skepticism and vigilance. The psychological impact of fraud can linger long after the financial losses have been recouped, hindering victims' ability to move forward and rebuild their lives.

Social Stigma

Financial fraud can carry a social stigma that further compounds the challenges faced by victims. Society's perception of victims as gullible or negligent can exacerbate feelings of shame and self-blame, deterring individuals from seeking support or speaking out about their experiences. The fear of judgment and ostracism may drive victims to suffer in silence, exacerbating their isolation and hindering their recovery process.

Rebuilding Trust

Rebuilding trust in oneself and others is a pivotal aspect of recovery from financial fraud. Victims may grapple with feelings of self-doubt and mistrust, questioning their own judgment and the motives of those around them. Restoring a sense of security and confidence in one's ability to make sound financial decisions is a gradual process that requires patience, resilience, and support from trusted allies.

Financial Literacy and Empowerment

Empowering victims with financial literacy and resources is essential in facilitating their recovery journey. Providing access to educational workshops, financial counseling, and support networks can equip victims with the knowledge and skills needed to regain control over their finances and make informed decisions. By fostering a sense of empowerment and self-reliance, victims can reclaim agency over their financial futures and mitigate the risk of falling prey to fraud again.

Community Support and Advocacy

Community support and advocacy play a crucial role in amplifying the voices of fraud victims and effecting positive change. Advocacy groups, nonprofit organizations, and grassroots movements can raise awareness about the prevalence and impact of financial fraud, advocate for policy reforms, and provide a platform for victims to share their stories and seek solidarity. By fostering a sense of solidarity and collective action, communities can empower victims, challenge societal attitudes toward fraud, and foster a culture of accountability and justice.

Holistic Healing

Recovery from financial fraud is not just about reclaiming lost assets; it's about healing on a holistic level - physically, emotionally, and psychologically. Holistic healing approaches, such as therapy, mindfulness practices, and support groups, can help victims address the underlying trauma of fraud, cultivate resilience, and foster a sense of renewal and purpose. By prioritizing self-care and holistic well-being, victims can transcend the role of mere survivors and emerge stronger, wiser, and more resilient than before.

Conclusion

Recovering from financial fraud is a multifaceted journey fraught with challenges, but it's also a testament to the resilience of the human spirit. By acknowledging the complexities of recovery and addressing the diverse needs of victims, we can pave the way for healing, empowerment, and justice. Together, we can build a more equitable and compassionate society where victims of financial fraud are not only supported but also empowered to thrive in the face of adversity.

Introduction

Financial fraud is not merely about monetary loss; it leaves a profound emotional scar on its victims. Among the myriad of emotions experienced, stigma and shame often reign supreme. In the shadows of deceit, victims grapple with these invisible burdens, hindering their ability to seek support and share their experiences. Understanding the intricacies of stigma and shame is paramount in comprehending the profound impact of financial fraud on its victims.

The Anatomy of Stigma

Stigma is a powerful force, capable of inflicting lasting damage on an individual's psyche. In the realm of financial fraud, victims are often unfairly branded as naive, careless, or even complicit in their own victimization. This societal judgment only serves to deepen their sense of shame and isolation. The stigma associated with being defrauded not only amplifies the emotional distress but also erects formidable barriers to seeking assistance.

The Weight of Shame

Shame is a visceral emotion, gnawing away at one's self-worth and dignity. Victims of financial fraud often internalize the shame, blaming themselves for their misfortune. The fear of being judged or ridiculed by others compounds this self-inflicted agony, driving victims further into silence. The pervasive nature of shame can corrode relationships, erode trust, and exacerbate the trauma of the fraud experience.

Breaking the Silence

The path to healing begins with breaking the silence surrounding financial fraud. Encouraging victims to share their stories in a safe and supportive environment is paramount. By fostering empathy and understanding, we can dismantle the walls of stigma and shame that imprison so many victims. Empowering individuals to speak out not only facilitates their own healing but also raises awareness about the prevalence and impact of financial fraud in our society.

Shifting the Narrative

Central to combating stigma and shame is reframing the narrative surrounding financial fraud. Instead of blaming the victim, we must hold perpetrators accountable for their actions. By shifting the focus from the shortcomings of the victim to the criminality of the fraudster, we can strip away the layers of stigma and shame that shroud the issue. Advocating for justice and restitution not only validates the experiences of victims but also sends a powerful message that fraud will not be tolerated.

Building a Supportive Ecosystem

Creating a supportive ecosystem is essential in mitigating the stigma and shame associated with financial fraud. This entails providing victims with access to comprehensive resources, including counseling, legal assistance, and peer support groups. By offering a holistic approach to recovery, we can empower victims to reclaim their sense of agency and resilience. Additionally, fostering collaboration between government agencies, financial institutions, and community organizations can strengthen the safety net for victims and enhance prevention efforts.

Educating the Public

Education is a powerful tool in dispelling myths and misconceptions surrounding financial fraud. By raising awareness about common tactics used by fraudsters and sharing real-life experiences of victims, we can empower individuals to recognize and report suspicious activities. Moreover, integrating financial literacy programs into school curricula can equip future generations with the knowledge and skills to protect themselves from fraud. By fostering a culture of vigilance and accountability, we can create a more resilient society that stands united against financial exploitation.

Conclusion

Stigma and shame are formidable adversaries in the fight against financial fraud. Yet, by shedding light on these invisible burdens and fostering a culture of empathy and support, we can empower victims to reclaim their voices and rebuild their lives. It is incumbent upon all of us to challenge the stigma, amplify the voices of victims, and work towards a future where financial fraud is no longer shrouded in silence and shame.

Introduction

Financial fraud wreaks havoc not only on victims' finances but also on their emotional well-being. Pursuing justice against fraudsters through legal action is often seen as a means of seeking recompense and closure. However, the journey through the legal system comes with its own set of challenges and costs. In this article, we delve into the intricate web of legal battles and the overwhelming financial burden it places on victims of financial fraud.

Understanding the Complexities of Legal Battles

Legal battles against perpetrators of financial fraud are intricate and multifaceted. From gathering evidence to navigating complex legal procedures, victims often find themselves embroiled in a prolonged and arduous process. The intricacies of financial laws and regulations further add layers of complexity, requiring expert legal counsel to navigate effectively.

The Emotional Toll

Beyond the financial implications, the emotional toll of legal battles cannot be overstated. Victims endure prolonged periods of stress, anxiety, and uncertainty as they await resolution. The emotional trauma of reliving the events of the fraud through court proceedings can exacerbate the already distressing situation, impacting victims' mental health and overall well-being.

Mounting Legal Fees

One of the most significant deterrents to pursuing legal action against fraudsters is the exorbitant cost involved. Legal fees, including attorney retainer fees, court filing fees, and expert witness fees, can quickly escalate, placing an immense financial strain on victims already grappling with the aftermath of financial loss. For many victims, the prospect of mounting legal fees becomes a barrier to seeking justice, forcing them to weigh the costs against the potential outcomes.

Lengthy Court Battles

Legal proceedings against fraudsters are notorious for their lengthy durations. Court dockets are often congested, leading to delays in scheduling hearings and trials. As a result, victims may find themselves embroiled in a protracted legal battle that spans months or even years. The prolonged uncertainty and prolonged legal process further exacerbate the financial and emotional burden on victims, prolonging their journey toward closure and resolution.

Navigating Legal Complexities

Navigating the legal complexities of financial fraud cases requires specialized expertise and resources. Victims must engage competent legal counsel with a deep understanding of financial laws and regulations. Moreover, the adversarial nature of litigation means that victims must be prepared to counter the defense's tactics and strategies, further adding to the intricacy of legal proceedings. Without proper guidance and support, victims may find themselves overwhelmed and ill-equipped to navigate the legal maze effectively.

Seeking Alternative Resolution

Given the formidable challenges and costs associated with pursuing legal action, some victims opt for alternative methods of resolution. Mediation and arbitration offer avenues for resolving disputes outside the courtroom, potentially reducing the financial and emotional burden on victims. While these alternative methods may offer a quicker and less adversarial means of resolution, they may not always result in the desired outcome for victims seeking recompense and justice.

The Importance of Victim Support

Amidst the legal battles and financial burdens, the importance of victim support cannot be overstated. Victims of financial fraud require not only legal guidance but also emotional support to navigate the challenges they face. Support groups, counseling services, and advocacy organizations play a crucial role in providing victims with the resources and assistance they need to cope with the aftermath of fraud and pursue justice effectively.

Conclusion

Legal battles against perpetrators of financial fraud entail significant financial and emotional burdens for victims. From mounting legal fees to lengthy court battles, the journey toward justice is fraught with challenges and complexities. Despite the formidable obstacles, victims are driven by a desire for recompense and closure. As we strive to understand the impact of financial fraud on victims, it is essential to recognize the toll of legal battles and the need for comprehensive support systems to aid victims in their pursuit of justice and healing.

Introduction

Financial fraud not only inflicts monetary losses but also leaves behind a trail of shattered lives. Among its myriad repercussions, one of the most profound is its impact on victims' careers and livelihoods. This article delves into the intricate ways financial fraud disrupts individuals' professional trajectories, jeopardizing their livelihoods and making it arduous to rebuild their lives.

The Genesis of Financial Fraud

Before delving into its ramifications, it's imperative to understand the essence of financial fraud. It encompasses a spectrum of deceitful practices, including Ponzi schemes, identity theft, embezzlement, and investment scams. Perpetrators exploit trust, manipulate financial systems, and prey on vulnerabilities, leaving victims in a state of profound distress.

Unraveling the Consequences

1. Economic Instability

Financial fraud strikes at the heart of economic stability. Victims often face sudden and substantial financial losses, depleting their savings and investments. This upheaval destabilizes their economic foundations, triggering a cascade of challenges that reverberate across various facets of their lives.

2. Career Disruption

The ramifications extend beyond financial losses. Many victims experience significant disruptions in their careers. Fraud-induced stress and anxiety may impede job performance, leading to decreased productivity and, in severe cases, job loss. The aftermath of fraud tarnishes professional reputations, undermining years of hard work and dedication.

3. Loss of Trust and Reputation

Trust, once shattered, is challenging to rebuild. Victims of financial fraud often endure reputational damage, both personally and professionally. Employers, colleagues, and business partners may harbor suspicions or skepticism, casting shadows over their integrity and competence. This erosion of trust can hinder career advancement opportunities and strain professional relationships.

4. Emotional Toll

The emotional toll of financial fraud is profound. Victims grapple with a myriad of emotions, including anger, betrayal, and shame. The psychological impact permeates every aspect of their lives, including their ability to focus on work and make sound professional decisions. Coping with trauma becomes a daunting task, exacerbating the challenges of maintaining career stability.

5. Legal Battles

Navigating the aftermath of financial fraud often entails protracted legal battles. Victims may find themselves embroiled in complex litigation processes, consuming valuable time and resources. Legal proceedings further exacerbate stress and uncertainty, compounding the challenges of rebuilding professional lives amidst turmoil.

6. Financial Obligations

The financial ramifications of fraud extend far beyond immediate losses. Victims may find themselves burdened with unexpected debts, legal fees, and restitution payments. Meeting financial obligations becomes a Herculean task, exacerbating the strain on already precarious livelihoods.

Rebuilding Lives: A Path Forward

Despite the formidable challenges posed by financial fraud, resilience prevails. Victims embark on a journey of rebuilding their lives, navigating obstacles with courage and determination.

1. Seeking Support

Central to the process of recovery is seeking support from trusted networks, including family, friends, and professional counselors. Sharing experiences and emotions in a supportive environment fosters healing and resilience.

2. Financial Rehabilitation

Recovering from financial fraud necessitates a comprehensive approach to financial rehabilitation. Victims may benefit from financial counseling, debt management strategies, and accessing resources for restitution or compensation.

3. Professional Redevelopment

Rebuilding professional lives requires perseverance and strategic planning. Victims can leverage their skills, expertise, and professional networks to explore new career opportunities or embark on entrepreneurial ventures. Investing in continuous learning and skill development enhances marketability and resilience in an ever-evolving job market.

4. Advocacy and Awareness

Empowering victims and raising awareness about the prevalence and impact of financial fraud are critical endeavors. Advocacy efforts aim to enact legislative reforms, strengthen consumer protections, and hold perpetrators accountable. Education and awareness initiatives equip individuals with knowledge and tools to safeguard against fraud and mitigate its consequences.

5. Embracing Resilience

Above all, resilience emerges as a guiding beacon in the aftermath of financial fraud. Embracing resilience entails cultivating inner strength, adapting to adversity, and embracing opportunities for growth and renewal. Through resilience, victims transcend the adversities wrought by fraud, emerging stronger and more resilient than before.

Conclusion

Financial fraud casts a long shadow, leaving victims grappling with profound economic, professional, and emotional ramifications. Its impact on careers and livelihoods reverberates far beyond monetary losses, challenging individuals to rebuild their lives amidst turmoil and uncertainty. Yet, amidst adversity, resilience prevails, illuminating a path forward towards healing, recovery, and renewal. As we strive to understand and confront the scourge of financial fraud, let us uphold compassion, solidarity, and unwavering resolve in supporting victims on their journey towards restoration and redemption.

Introduction

Financial fraud inflicts a profound impact not only on the victims' financial stability but also on their emotional and psychological well-being. The aftermath of falling prey to financial scams can be devastating, leaving victims grappling with a myriad of emotions ranging from anger and betrayal to shame and despair. Coping with the aftermath of financial fraud requires resilience and support from various sources. In this article, we delve into coping mechanisms and support systems essential for victims to navigate the challenges of recovery.

Understanding the Emotional Toll

Financial fraud is not merely a monetary loss; it's a betrayal of trust that can shatter one's sense of security and self-worth. Victims often experience a whirlwind of emotions, including shock, disbelief, anger, guilt, and embarrassment. The realization that they've been deceived can lead to a profound sense of betrayal, impacting their ability to trust others in the future.

Coping Mechanisms

1. Acknowledging Emotions: The first step in coping with the aftermath of financial fraud is acknowledging and accepting the emotions that accompany the experience. Denying or suppressing these feelings can prolong the healing process. Victims should allow themselves to feel whatever emotions arise without judgment.

2. Seeking Support: **Sharing one's experience with trusted friends, family members, or support groups can provide immense emotional relief. Talking about the ordeal can help victims process their emotions and gain perspective from others who have been through similar experiences.**

3. Practicing Self-Care: **Engaging in self-care activities such as exercise, meditation, or pursuing hobbies can help alleviate stress and promote emotional well-being. Taking time to rest, eat healthily, and prioritize self-care is crucial for rebuilding resilience.**

4. Setting Boundaries: **Victims may find it necessary to establish boundaries with family members, friends, or acquaintances who may inadvertently exacerbate their distress by offering unsolicited advice or insensitive remarks. Learning to assertively communicate one's needs and limits is essential for self-preservation.**

5. Seeking Professional Help: **In some cases, the emotional impact of financial fraud may be overwhelming, necessitating professional intervention. Therapists or counselors experienced in trauma and financial abuse can provide invaluable support and guidance in processing emotions and developing coping strategies.**

Support Systems

1. Legal Assistance: **Victims of financial fraud may benefit from seeking legal assistance to explore their options for restitution or pursuing legal action against the perpetrators. Legal professionals specializing in financial fraud can offer expert advice and representation throughout the legal process.**

2. Financial Counseling: Rebuilding financial stability after falling victim to fraud can be daunting. Financial counselors or advisors can help victims assess their financial situation, develop a realistic budget, and formulate a plan for regaining control of their finances.

3. Victim Support Groups: Joining support groups specifically tailored to victims of financial fraud can provide a sense of solidarity and belonging. Connecting with others who have undergone similar experiences can offer validation, empathy, and practical advice for coping and recovery.

4. Community Resources: Many communities offer resources and services for victims of financial fraud, ranging from crisis hotlines to financial assistance programs. These resources can provide vital support in times of crisis and help victims access the assistance they need to navigate the challenges of recovery.

5. Family and Friends: The support of loved ones can be a cornerstone of recovery for victims of financial fraud. Family and friends can offer emotional support, practical assistance, and a listening ear during difficult times. Building and nurturing these relationships is essential for healing and resilience.

Conclusion

Coping with the aftermath of financial fraud is a challenging journey that requires resilience, support, and self-care. By acknowledging their emotions, seeking support from various sources, and accessing available resources, victims can navigate the complexities of recovery and emerge stronger and more resilient. It's essential for society as a whole to recognize the emotional toll of financial fraud and provide the necessary support systems to assist victims in their journey toward healing and financial recovery.

Chapter 12. Financial Literacy and Empowerment

Introduction

In today's complex financial landscape, the prevalence of fraud poses a significant threat to individuals and communities worldwide. Financial fraud, ranging from investment scams to identity theft, can have devastating consequences for victims, leading to financial ruin, emotional distress, and shattered trust. However, amidst this adversity lies a powerful tool for protection: financial literacy. By equipping individuals with the knowledge and skills to understand, manage, and navigate financial matters, we can empower them to recognize warning signs, make informed decisions, and safeguard themselves against fraud.

Understanding Financial Literacy

Financial literacy encompasses a broad spectrum of competencies, including budgeting, saving, investing, debt management, and understanding financial products and services. At its core, it involves the ability to effectively manage one's finances, make informed decisions, and plan for the future. Unfortunately, studies consistently show that a significant portion of the population lacks basic financial knowledge, leaving them vulnerable to exploitation by fraudsters.

The Importance of Financial Literacy in Fraud Prevention

Empowering individuals with financial literacy is essential for fraud prevention on multiple fronts. Firstly, it enables individuals to recognize common red flags and tactics used by fraudsters. Whether it's an unsolicited investment opportunity promising unrealistic returns or a phishing email requesting sensitive personal information, a financially literate individual is better equipped to discern legitimate financial opportunities from fraudulent schemes.

Secondly, financial literacy enhances individuals' ability to make sound financial decisions. By understanding the principles of risk and reward, diversification, and due diligence, individuals can evaluate potential investments and financial products more critically, reducing the likelihood of falling prey to fraudulent schemes promising quick riches or unrealistic benefits.

Moreover, financial literacy fosters a sense of empowerment and confidence in managing one's finances. When individuals possess the knowledge and skills to create and adhere to a budget, build savings, and navigate financial institutions, they are less susceptible to manipulation by fraudsters seeking to exploit their financial insecurities or ignorance.

Promoting Financial Literacy for Fraud Prevention

Efforts to promote financial literacy must be comprehensive, reaching individuals across all age groups, socioeconomic backgrounds, and educational levels. Schools play a crucial role in laying the foundation for financial literacy through structured education programs that teach basic financial concepts from an early age.

However, financial education should not end with formal schooling. Continuous learning opportunities, such as workshops, seminars, online resources, and community programs, are essential for reinforcing and expanding financial knowledge throughout life.

Furthermore, financial institutions, government agencies, and nonprofit organizations have a responsibility to provide accessible and unbiased financial education resources to the public. Whether through informational websites, educational materials, or personalized counseling services, these entities can empower individuals to take control of their financial futures and protect themselves from fraud.

In addition to education, the integration of technology can enhance financial literacy efforts and reach broader audiences. Mobile apps, interactive online courses, and gamified learning platforms offer engaging and accessible ways to teach financial concepts and promote healthy financial habits.

Overcoming Barriers to Financial Literacy

While promoting financial literacy is crucial for fraud prevention, it's essential to acknowledge and address the barriers that hinder individuals from accessing and engaging with financial education. These barriers may include socioeconomic factors, cultural norms, language barriers, and limited access to resources in underserved communities.

To overcome these barriers, collaborative efforts are needed from policymakers, financial institutions, community organizations, and educators. Initiatives such as targeted outreach programs, culturally sensitive curriculum development, and partnerships with community leaders can help bridge the gap and ensure that financial education reaches those who need it most.

Moreover, efforts to promote financial literacy should prioritize inclusivity and diversity, recognizing the unique needs and challenges faced by different demographic groups. Tailoring educational materials and outreach strategies to resonate with diverse audiences can enhance engagement and effectiveness.

Empowering Individuals Through Financial Literacy

In conclusion, financial literacy serves as a powerful tool for empowering individuals to protect themselves against financial fraud. By equipping people with the knowledge, skills, and confidence to manage their finances effectively, we can mitigate the risk of falling victim to fraudulent schemes and promote financial well-being and resilience.

However, achieving widespread financial literacy requires concerted efforts from policymakers, educators, financial institutions, and communities. By investing in comprehensive education initiatives, leveraging technology, and addressing barriers to access, we can ensure that everyone has the opportunity to build a solid foundation of financial knowledge and make informed decisions that safeguard their financial futures.

Ultimately, by advocating for increased financial literacy, we can empower individuals to take control of their financial lives, recognize and avoid fraudulent schemes, and build a more secure and prosperous future for themselves and their communities.

Introduction

Financial fraud is not just a crime against individuals; it ripples through communities, leaving a trail of devastation that extends far beyond the immediate victims. In this article, we delve into the profound impact financial fraud can have on communities, exploring its economic, social, and psychological consequences. From economic downturns to the erosion of trust in local businesses, understanding these effects is crucial in combating financial fraud effectively.

Economic Downturns

One of the most significant community-level impacts of financial fraud is its contribution to economic downturns. When individuals fall victim to fraudulent schemes, they often suffer substantial financial losses, impacting their ability to contribute to the local economy. These losses can lead to reduced consumer spending, lower investment in businesses, and ultimately, a slowdown in economic growth. Moreover, the financial strain on victims may result in job losses or the closure of small businesses, further exacerbating the economic downturn within the community.

Loss of Trust in Local Businesses

Financial fraud erodes trust, not only in the perpetrators but also in the broader business community. When individuals are swindled out of their hard-earned money by fraudulent schemes, they become wary of engaging with local businesses, fearing that they too may fall victim to deceit.

This loss of trust can have far-reaching consequences, affecting the livelihoods of honest entrepreneurs and undermining the foundation of community-based commerce. Moreover, the tarnished reputation of local businesses may deter external investment, hindering economic development and growth.

Social Disruption

Beyond its economic ramifications, financial fraud can disrupt the social fabric of communities. Victims of fraud often experience feelings of betrayal, shame, and isolation, leading to strained relationships with family, friends, and neighbors. The psychological toll of financial fraud can be profound, causing stress, anxiety, and depression among victims and their families. Additionally, communities may experience increased tension and conflict as individuals grapple with the fallout of fraudulent schemes, further undermining social cohesion and trust.

Impact on Vulnerable Populations

Financial fraud disproportionately affects vulnerable populations within communities, exacerbating existing inequalities. Elderly individuals, immigrants, and low-income families are often targeted by fraudsters due to their perceived financial vulnerability and lack of access to resources and support networks. When these marginalized groups fall victim to financial fraud, the impact reverberates throughout the entire community, perpetuating cycles of poverty and disenfranchisement.

Undermining Community Resilience

Communities rely on trust, cooperation, and resilience to thrive in the face of challenges. However, financial fraud erodes these essential pillars, weakening the community's ability to respond effectively to crises. As trust in institutions and fellow community members wanes, individuals may become more hesitant to seek help or support, further isolating themselves from potential assistance. This breakdown in community resilience can prolong the recovery process, making it harder for affected individuals to rebuild their lives and livelihoods.

Challenges in Combatting Financial Fraud

Combatting financial fraud requires a multifaceted approach that addresses both prevention and enforcement. However, several challenges hinder effective action against fraudulent activities at the community level. Limited resources, lack of awareness, and complex jurisdictional issues often impede efforts to identify and prosecute fraudsters. Moreover, the rapid evolution of technology has enabled fraudsters to perpetrate sophisticated schemes across geographical boundaries, making detection and prevention even more challenging.

Building Community Resilience

Despite these challenges, there are steps communities can take to mitigate the impact of financial fraud and build resilience against future threats. Education and awareness campaigns can empower individuals to recognize and avoid fraudulent schemes, reducing the pool of potential victims. Community-based support networks and resources can provide assistance to those affected by fraud, helping them navigate the aftermath and rebuild their lives. Collaboration between law enforcement, government agencies, and community organizations is essential in identifying and prosecuting fraudsters, deterring future criminal activity, and restoring trust in local institutions.

Conclusion

Financial fraud exacts a heavy toll on communities, undermining economic stability, social cohesion, and trust in local businesses. Its impact reverberates through every aspect of community life, affecting individuals, families, and businesses alike. By understanding the broader ripple effects of financial fraud and taking proactive steps to combat it, communities can build resilience, protect vulnerable populations, and foster trust and cooperation among their members. Only through collective action and collaboration can we effectively confront the scourge of financial fraud and safeguard the well-being of our communities for generations to come.

Introduction

Financial fraud is a pervasive issue that affects individuals across all demographics, but one group particularly vulnerable to its devastating effects is the elderly population. As advancements in technology continue to reshape the financial landscape, older adults find themselves increasingly susceptible to various forms of exploitation and scams. In this article, we delve into the unique vulnerabilities faced by elderly individuals regarding financial fraud and highlight the necessity for targeted support and protection measures.

Understanding Elderly Vulnerability

Elderly individuals are often targeted by fraudsters due to a combination of factors that make them more susceptible to manipulation. One significant factor is cognitive decline, which is a natural part of the aging process. As individuals age, they may experience a decline in cognitive abilities such as memory, processing speed, and decision-making skills. These changes can impair their ability to discern fraudulent schemes and make them more likely to fall victim to scams.

Furthermore, elderly individuals may experience social isolation, either due to retirement, the loss of friends and family members, or physical limitations that restrict their mobility. This isolation can make them more susceptible to manipulation as fraudsters exploit their loneliness and desire for social interaction.

Another contributing factor to elderly vulnerability is financial insecurity. Many older adults are living on fixed incomes, relying on retirement savings, pensions, and social security benefits to meet their financial needs. Fraudsters often target individuals who are experiencing financial difficulties, promising them quick fixes or unrealistic investment opportunities.

Exploitation Tactics

Fraudsters employ various tactics to exploit elderly individuals and defraud them of their hard-earned money. One common tactic is impersonation scams, where fraudsters pose as representatives from legitimate organizations such as banks, government agencies, or utility companies. They use fear tactics or false promises to coerce elderly individuals into providing personal information or transferring funds.

Another prevalent form of exploitation is investment fraud, where fraudsters offer elderly individuals fraudulent investment opportunities promising high returns with little to no risk. These schemes often involve complex financial products or Ponzi schemes designed to deceive investors and enrich the fraudsters.

Additionally, telemarketing scams targeting the elderly are widespread, where fraudsters use high-pressure sales tactics to convince older adults to purchase overpriced or nonexistent products or services. These scams can result in significant financial losses and emotional distress for the victims.

The Need for Targeted Support and Protection

Given the unique vulnerabilities faced by elderly individuals regarding financial fraud, there is an urgent need for targeted support and protection measures to safeguard this vulnerable population. One essential aspect of addressing this issue is education and awareness. Providing elderly individuals with information about common scams and fraud prevention strategies can empower them to recognize and avoid fraudulent schemes.

Furthermore, community outreach programs and support networks can play a crucial role in combating elderly exploitation. These programs provide older adults with social engagement opportunities, reducing their susceptibility to isolation and loneliness, which are often exploited by fraudsters.

Legal and regulatory frameworks also play a vital role in protecting elderly individuals from financial exploitation. Implementing stricter regulations on financial institutions and enforcing harsher penalties for perpetrators of financial fraud can serve as a deterrent and provide recourse for victims.

Moreover, financial institutions can enhance their efforts to detect and prevent fraud targeting elderly customers by implementing robust security measures and monitoring systems. Providing elderly customers with personalized assistance and support can also help mitigate their vulnerability to exploitation.

Conclusion

Elderly individuals are particularly vulnerable to financial fraud due to a combination of factors such as cognitive decline, social isolation, and financial insecurity. Fraudsters exploit these vulnerabilities using various tactics to defraud older adults of their savings and assets. To address this issue, targeted support and protection measures are essential, including education and awareness initiatives, community outreach programs, legal and regulatory frameworks, and enhanced efforts by financial institutions. By working together to protect elderly individuals from financial exploitation, we can help ensure their financial security and well-being in their golden years.

Introduction

Financial fraud has become a pervasive issue in today's society, affecting millions of individuals worldwide. While the impacts of financial fraud are often discussed in terms of financial loss and legal consequences, it's crucial to recognize the profound influence that cultural and socioeconomic factors exert on victims. This article delves into the intricate relationship between cultural norms, socioeconomic status, and their role in shaping individuals' susceptibility to financial fraud and their ability to recover from its aftermath.

Cultural Norms and Financial Behavior

Culture plays a significant role in shaping individuals' attitudes towards money and financial decisions. Cultural norms regarding trust, risk-taking, and interpersonal relationships can either mitigate or exacerbate the risk of falling victim to financial fraud. In cultures where trust is highly valued and skepticism towards others is low, individuals may be more susceptible to schemes that exploit their trust.

Furthermore, cultural attitudes towards wealth and material success can influence individuals' susceptibility to fraudulent schemes promising quick and substantial returns. In societies that prioritize material wealth and social status, individuals may be more inclined to take financial risks in pursuit of perceived opportunities for financial gain, making them vulnerable to fraudulent schemes.

Socioeconomic Status and Vulnerability

Socioeconomic status plays a crucial role in determining an individual's vulnerability to financial fraud. Lower-income individuals and families are often disproportionately affected by financial fraud due to limited access to resources, financial education, and legal recourse. Economic desperation and financial instability can make individuals more susceptible to fraudulent schemes promising relief from financial hardship or offering unrealistic financial opportunities.

Moreover, individuals from lower socioeconomic backgrounds may lack the financial literacy necessary to discern legitimate investment opportunities from fraudulent schemes. Limited access to formal financial institutions and services may also leave these individuals more vulnerable to exploitation by fraudulent actors operating outside the regulated financial system.

Psychological Impact and Recovery

The impact of financial fraud extends far beyond monetary loss, often causing significant psychological distress and emotional trauma for victims. Cultural and socioeconomic factors can influence the severity of these psychological effects and individuals' ability to cope and recover from the trauma of being defrauded.

Cultural stigma surrounding financial failure and victim blaming can exacerbate the psychological distress experienced by fraud victims, preventing them from seeking support and assistance. In some cultures, the shame associated with being deceived or losing money may deter victims from reporting the fraud or seeking help, further isolating them from potential sources of support.

Socioeconomic disparities also play a critical role in shaping individuals' ability to recover from financial fraud. Higher-income individuals may have greater access to financial resources, social support networks, and mental health services, facilitating their recovery process. Conversely, lower-income individuals may face greater challenges in rebuilding their financial security and emotional well-being following a fraudulent incident.

Cultural Considerations in Recovery

Cultural competence is essential in providing effective support and assistance to victims of financial fraud. Recognizing and respecting cultural norms, beliefs, and values is crucial in addressing the unique needs and challenges faced by victims from diverse cultural backgrounds.

Culturally sensitive outreach and support services can help break down barriers to reporting and seeking assistance among marginalized communities. Providing culturally relevant resources and interventions tailored to the specific cultural context can empower victims to navigate the recovery process more effectively and rebuild their trust and confidence in financial institutions and systems.

Socioeconomic Support and Empowerment

Addressing the socioeconomic factors that contribute to vulnerability to financial fraud requires a multifaceted approach aimed at addressing systemic inequalities and empowering marginalized communities.

Enhancing access to financial education and literacy programs, particularly among lower-income and underserved populations, can help individuals develop the knowledge and skills necessary to protect themselves from financial fraud and make informed financial decisions.

Additionally, efforts to improve economic stability and social support systems can help mitigate the impact of financial fraud on vulnerable individuals and families. Investing in affordable housing, healthcare, and social welfare programs can help address underlying economic disparities and provide a safety net for those at risk of financial exploitation.

Conclusion

Understanding the complex interplay between cultural norms, socioeconomic status, and financial fraud is essential for developing effective strategies to prevent fraud and support victims. By addressing the cultural and socioeconomic factors that contribute to vulnerability and influence recovery, we can work towards creating a more equitable and resilient financial system that protects all individuals from the devastating impact of financial fraud.

Introduction

Financial fraud can have devastating consequences for its victims, leaving them feeling helpless, betrayed, and financially vulnerable. In the wake of such fraudulent activities, it's crucial for victims to know that they are not alone and that there are support services and resources available to assist them in navigating through the aftermath. In this article, we will explore various support services and resources tailored to help victims of financial fraud cope, recover, and seek justice.

Victim Advocacy Organizations

Victim advocacy organizations play a vital role in supporting individuals who have fallen victim to financial fraud. These organizations offer a range of services aimed at empowering victims and helping them understand their rights and options. They provide emotional support, guidance through legal proceedings, and assistance in accessing other resources.

One notable organization is the National Center for Victims of Crime (NCVC) in the United States, which offers a wide array of services for victims of all types of crimes, including financial fraud. They provide support hotlines, online resources, and referrals to local victim assistance programs. Additionally, they advocate for victims' rights and work to improve policies and laws related to victim assistance.

Similarly, the Financial Industry Regulatory Authority (FINRA) in the United States operates the Securities

Helpline for Seniors, a resource specifically designed to assist senior investors who have been victims of financial fraud or exploitation. The helpline offers support, guidance, and referrals to relevant agencies and services.

Financial Counseling Services

Financial fraud can have significant implications for a victim's financial well-being, often leaving them facing substantial losses and uncertainty about their financial future. Financial counseling services can be instrumental in helping victims regain control of their finances and develop strategies for rebuilding their financial security.

Non-profit organizations such as the National Foundation for Credit Counseling (NFCC) in the United States offer free or low-cost financial counseling services to individuals facing financial challenges, including those resulting from fraud. Certified financial counselors work with victims to assess their financial situation, create personalized financial plans, and provide guidance on managing debt, budgeting, and rebuilding credit.

Additionally, many local community organizations and religious institutions offer financial counseling services to members of their communities. These services may include workshops, seminars, and one-on-one counseling sessions tailored to address the specific needs of financial fraud victims.

Legal Aid Services

Seeking legal recourse can be a daunting task for victims of financial fraud, especially if they lack the financial resources to hire a private attorney. Legal aid services provide free or low-cost legal assistance to individuals who cannot afford private representation, ensuring that all victims have access to justice regardless of their financial circumstances.

Legal aid organizations, such as Legal Aid Society in the United States, offer a range of legal services to victims of financial fraud, including assistance with filing complaints, negotiating settlements, and representing clients in court proceedings. They may also provide referrals to pro bono attorneys or other legal resources.

Moreover, government agencies such as the Consumer Financial Protection Bureau (CFPB) in the United States offer resources and assistance to consumers who have been victims of financial fraud. The CFPB provides information on consumer rights, complaint filing procedures, and legal options for recourse against fraudulent practices by financial institutions.

Psychological Counseling and Support Groups

In addition to the financial impact, victims of financial fraud often experience emotional distress, including feelings of shame, anger, and anxiety. Psychological counseling and support groups can offer victims a safe space to process their emotions, share their experiences, and receive support from others who have gone through similar situations.

Many mental health professionals, including psychologists and social workers, specialize in working with victims of crime and trauma. They can provide individual counseling sessions to help victims cope with the emotional aftermath of financial fraud and develop healthy coping strategies.

Furthermore, support groups, both in-person and online, offer victims the opportunity to connect with others who have experienced financial fraud. These groups provide peer support, practical advice, and a sense of community, which can be invaluable in the recovery process.

Government Assistance Programs

Various government assistance programs exist to provide financial support and assistance to victims of crime, including financial fraud. These programs may offer compensation for out-of-pocket expenses related to the crime, such as medical bills, counseling fees, and lost wages.

For example, the Victims of Crime Act (VOCA) in the United States provides funding to states and territories to support victim assistance and compensation programs. Victims can apply for compensation to cover expenses resulting from financial fraud, such as legal fees and medical costs.

Additionally, government agencies may offer specialized assistance programs for specific types of financial fraud, such as identity theft or investment scams. These programs may provide resources, educational materials, and assistance with resolving issues related to the fraud.

Conclusion

Victims of financial fraud have access to a range of support services and resources to help them cope, recover, and seek justice. From victim advocacy organizations and financial counseling services to legal aid assistance and psychological counseling, these resources are essential in empowering victims and assisting them in navigating through the challenges posed by financial fraud. It is crucial for victims to be aware of these resources and to reach out for support when needed. By utilizing these services, victims can take proactive steps towards healing and rebuilding their lives in the aftermath of financial fraud.

Introduction

Financial fraud is a pervasive and detrimental crime that not only undermines trust in financial systems but also inflicts significant harm on its victims. From investment scams to identity theft, the ramifications of financial fraud are far-reaching, affecting individuals, families, businesses, and even entire economies. As we delve into the complexities of understanding financial fraud's impact on victims, it becomes imperative to explore policy implications and advocate for reforms aimed at bolstering support for victims, strengthening enforcement measures, and enhancing consumer protections.

Understanding the Scope of Financial Fraud

Before delving into policy implications and reform, it's crucial to grasp the multifaceted nature of financial fraud. It encompasses a wide array of deceptive practices, including Ponzi schemes, insider trading, credit card fraud, and cybercrimes. Victims of financial fraud often suffer not only financial losses but also emotional distress, reputational damage, and a sense of betrayal. Furthermore, vulnerable populations, such as the elderly and low-income individuals, are disproportionately targeted, exacerbating social inequalities.

Policy Implications for Supporting Victims

One of the foremost policy implications in combating financial fraud is to prioritize support for victims. This entails establishing comprehensive victim assistance programs that provide financial counseling, legal aid, and mental health services. Moreover, fostering collaboration among law enforcement agencies, financial institutions, and consumer advocacy groups is essential for effectively addressing victims' needs and facilitating their recovery. Additionally, policymakers should allocate adequate resources to educate the public about common fraud schemes and empower individuals to recognize warning signs and protect themselves from falling prey to fraudulent activities.

Reforming Enforcement Measures

To deter financial fraud and hold perpetrators accountable, reforms in enforcement measures are imperative. This includes strengthening regulatory frameworks, enhancing surveillance systems, and imposing stricter penalties for fraudulent behavior. Regulatory agencies must be equipped with sufficient authority and resources to investigate suspicious activities promptly and prosecute offenders effectively. Moreover, international cooperation is crucial in combating cross-border financial crimes, necessitating the harmonization of legal standards and the sharing of intelligence among jurisdictions. By bolstering enforcement measures, policymakers can send a clear message that financial fraud will not be tolerated and perpetrators will face severe consequences for their actions.

Enhancing Consumer Protections

In addition to supporting victims and strengthening enforcement, policymakers must focus on enhancing consumer protections to prevent financial fraud. This involves implementing robust safeguards, such as stringent identity verification procedures, encryption technologies, and fraud detection systems, to safeguard individuals' financial information and mitigate the risk of data breaches.

Furthermore, promoting transparency and accountability within financial institutions is essential for building trust and ensuring that consumers are adequately informed about the products and services they engage with. Additionally, empowering regulatory agencies to enforce compliance with consumer protection laws and impose sanctions on entities that engage in deceptive practices is critical for safeguarding consumers' rights and interests.

Conclusion

Addressing the impact of financial fraud on victims requires a multifaceted approach that encompasses policy implications and reform across various domains. By prioritizing support for victims, strengthening enforcement measures, and enhancing consumer protections, policymakers can mitigate the devastating effects of financial fraud and foster a more resilient and secure financial ecosystem. It is imperative that policymakers collaborate with stakeholders from both the public and private sectors to enact meaningful reforms that uphold integrity, promote accountability, and safeguard the interests of consumers and investors alike. Only through concerted efforts and proactive measures can we effectively combat financial fraud and create a safer and more equitable financial landscape for all.

Introduction

Financial fraud is a global menace that not only undermines the stability of financial systems but also wreaks havoc on the lives of individuals who fall victim to it. From Ponzi schemes to identity theft and cyber fraud, the methods employed by fraudsters continue to evolve, making it crucial for nations to adopt effective strategies to support victims. However, approaches to victim support vary significantly across countries, reflecting differences in legal frameworks, cultural norms, and resource availability. In this article, we delve into the international perspectives on victim support, comparing strategies employed in various countries, highlighting best practices, and identifying areas for improvement.

United States

In the United States, victim support for financial fraud is facilitated through a combination of legal measures and victim services. The legal framework provides avenues for victims to seek restitution and pursue justice through criminal and civil litigation. Additionally, federal agencies such as the Federal Trade Commission (FTC) and the Consumer Financial Protection Bureau (CFPB) offer resources and assistance to victims of financial crimes.

Moreover, non-profit organizations and victim advocacy groups play a crucial role in providing emotional support, financial counseling, and legal assistance to victims. For example, the National Center for Victims of Crime offers a comprehensive range of services, including a hotline for victims to report fraud and access support services.

Best Practice: The Victim Compensation Program, available in many states, provides financial assistance to victims of crime, including those affected by financial fraud, to cover medical expenses, counseling, and lost wages.

Area for Improvement: Despite robust legal and support frameworks, coordination among various agencies and organizations could be enhanced to ensure seamless assistance to victims across different jurisdictions.

United Kingdom

In the United Kingdom, victim support initiatives focus not only on assisting victims after the occurrence of fraud but also on preventing fraud and raising awareness about scams. Organizations such as Action Fraud provide a centralized reporting mechanism for victims to report fraud and receive advice on how to protect themselves from future scams.

Furthermore, the UK government invests in educational campaigns to empower individuals with the knowledge and skills to recognize and avoid fraudulent schemes. Initiatives like the Take Five campaign educate the public about common tactics used by fraudsters and promote skepticism towards unsolicited communication requesting personal or financial information.

Best Practice: The Victim Support helpline offers emotional support and practical assistance to victims of all types of crime, including financial fraud, ensuring that victims have access to a wide range of support services.

: Despite efforts to raise awareness, there is a need for targeted outreach to vulnerable populations, such as the elderly and immigrant communities, who may be disproportionately targeted by fraudsters.

Japan

In Japan, victim support for financial fraud often relies on community-based networks and informal channels of assistance. While there are government agencies and non-profit organizations that offer support services, such as the National Consumer Affairs Center of Japan, community organizations such as neighborhood associations and local NGOs also play a significant role in providing assistance to victims.

These community-based support networks offer a personalized approach to victim support, leveraging existing social ties and cultural norms to provide emotional and practical assistance to victims. Volunteers often serve as mediators between victims and authorities, helping victims navigate bureaucratic processes and access necessary resources.

Best Practice: The Victim Support Centers established across Japan provide counseling, legal advice, and mediation services to victims of various crimes, including financial fraud, in a culturally sensitive manner.

Area for Improvement: Despite the strengths of community-based support networks, there may be gaps in services for victims who are not connected to existing community organizations or who face barriers to accessing assistance due to language or cultural differences.

Australia

Australia adopts a multidisciplinary approach to victim support, involving collaboration between government agencies, law enforcement, legal services, and community organizations. Victim Support Units within police departments offer immediate assistance to victims, including crisis intervention and referrals to support services.

Moreover, victim impact statements allow victims to express the emotional, financial, and psychological toll of fraud during sentencing hearings, ensuring that their voices are heard in the criminal justice process. Empowerment-focused programs, such as the Victims of Crime Assistance Tribunal, provide financial compensation and support services to help victims recover and rebuild their lives.

Best Practice: The Financial Ombudsman Service offers an alternative dispute resolution mechanism for victims of financial fraud to resolve disputes with financial institutions, providing a more accessible and efficient avenue for seeking redress.

Area for Improvement: Despite efforts to empower victims, there is a need for greater recognition of the long-term impacts of financial fraud and the provision of ongoing support services to facilitate recovery and resilience.

Conclusion

Across different countries, victim support for financial fraud varies in terms of legal frameworks, support services, and cultural approaches. While some countries prioritize legal remedies and comprehensive victim services, others emphasize prevention, community-based support, or victim empowerment. By comparing international perspectives on victim support, we can identify best practices and areas for improvement, ultimately working towards more effective and holistic strategies to combat financial fraud and support its victims on a global scale.

Introduction

Financial fraud can leave deep scars, not only on one's finances but also on their emotional well-being, relationships, and trust in institutions. However, amidst the devastation, there lies the potential for resilience, personal growth, and finding meaning beyond the fraudulent experience. In this final chapter, we explore the journey of rebuilding one's life after experiencing financial fraud, offering guidance and insights to empower victims to reclaim their lives and move forward.

Understanding Resilience

Resilience is the ability to bounce back from adversity, to adapt and thrive in the face of challenges. It's not about avoiding pain or pretending everything is fine; rather, it's about harnessing inner strength, seeking support, and finding ways to overcome obstacles. Building resilience is a gradual process that involves self-reflection, acceptance, and proactive steps towards healing.

Embracing Personal Growth

The aftermath of financial fraud presents an opportunity for personal growth and transformation. It's a chance to reassess priorities, cultivate resilience, and discover newfound strengths. Through self-discovery and introspection, victims can redefine their identity beyond the fraud experience, tapping into their inner resilience to navigate the complexities of recovery.

Finding Meaning Beyond the Fraud Experience

While financial fraud can shatter one's sense of security and trust, it can also inspire profound introspection and a reevaluation of life's purpose. By reframing the experience as a catalyst for growth and resilience, victims can find meaning in their journey, whether through advocating for change, helping others navigate similar challenges, or simply cherishing moments of joy and connection amidst adversity.

Rebuilding Trust

Rebuilding trust, both in oneself and others, is a crucial aspect of the recovery process. It requires patience, forgiveness, and a willingness to open oneself up to vulnerability. By surrounding oneself with supportive relationships and gradually extending trust to trustworthy individuals and institutions, victims can slowly rebuild the foundation of trust that was shattered by the fraud.

Financial Recovery Strategies

Financial recovery after fraud often involves a combination of practical steps and emotional healing. This may include working with financial advisors to regain control over finances, exploring legal avenues for restitution, and developing a sustainable financial plan for the future. Additionally, seeking counseling or therapy can help address the emotional toll of the fraud and cultivate resilience in the face of financial challenges.

Cultivating Self-Care

Self-care is paramount in the journey towards resilience and moving forward. This involves prioritizing one's physical, emotional, and mental well-being, whether through mindfulness practices, engaging in hobbies and activities that bring joy, or seeking professional support when needed. By nurturing oneself with compassion and kindness, victims can replenish their energy and resilience for the road ahead.

Fostering Meaningful Connections

Social support is a cornerstone of resilience, providing comfort, validation, and practical assistance during times of adversity. By fostering meaningful connections with friends, family, support groups, or online communities, victims can feel less isolated and gain perspective from others who have walked similar paths. Sharing experiences, insights, and resources can offer hope and encouragement on the journey towards healing.

Empowering Through Advocacy

Advocating for change and raising awareness about the impact of financial fraud can be a powerful way to reclaim agency and find meaning in the aftermath of victimization. By sharing their stories, speaking out against injustice, and advocating for policy reforms, victims can channel their experiences into a force for positive change, empowering themselves and others to prevent future fraud and support those affected by it.

Embracing Resilience as a Journey

Resilience is not a destination but a journey - a continuous process of growth, adaptation, and renewal. It's about embracing the ebb and flow of life's challenges, finding strength in vulnerability, and learning to thrive despite adversity. As victims of financial fraud embark on their journey towards resilience and moving forward, may they find solace in the knowledge that they are not alone, and that within every setback lies the seeds of resilience, hope, and possibility.

"Understanding Financial Fraud's Impact on Victims" delves deep into the multifaceted repercussions of financial fraud, offering a comprehensive examination across nineteen insightful chapters. From dissecting various fraud types like Pyramid Schemes to discussing the emotional turmoil victims endure, each chapter meticulously dissects the mechanics, consequences, and recovery challenges associated with financial fraud. It illuminates the devastating effects on victims' financial stability, mental health, relationships, and trust in institutions. From the stigma of victimhood to the complexities of legal battles, the book navigates through the intricate web of challenges victims face. Yet, it also offers a beacon of hope, emphasizing coping mechanisms, the importance of financial literacy, and the resilience needed to rebuild lives shattered by fraud. With a global perspective and a call for policy reforms, this book serves as both a scholarly resource and a guiding light for those navigating the aftermath of financial fraud.

ABOUT THE AUTHOR

Mr. C. P. Kumar is a retired Scientist 'G' from National Institute of Hydrology, Roorkee, Uttarakhand, India. He is also a Reiki Healer and Chakra Balancing practitioner (with pendulum dowsing) and offers Emotional Freedom Technique (EFT) to help individuals with emotional issues. Mr. Kumar has authored many books on technical, spiritual, and social topics.

For further details, you may visit his webpage
https://www.angelfire.com/nh/cpkumar/virgo.html